This is my
dump truck

Written by Chris Oxlade
Photography by Andy Crawford

SEA-TO-SEA

Mankato Collingwood London

This edition first published in 2008 by
Sea-to-Sea Publications
1980 Lookout Drive
North Mankato
Minnesota 56003

Printed in China

Library of Congress Cataloging in Publication Data

Oxlade, Chris.
   This is my dump truck / by Chris Oxlade.
      p.cm.
   ISBN 978-1-59771-105-0
   1. Earthmoving machinery--Juvenile literature. 2. Dump trucks--Juvenile literature. I.
Title.

TA725.O95 2007
621.8'65--dc22

                                    2006051283

9 8 7 6 5 4 3 2

Published by arrangement with the Watts Publishing Group Ltd, London.

Editor: Jennifer Schofield
Designer: Jemima Lumley
Photography: Andy Crawford
Dump truck driver: Peter Higton

Acknowledgments:
Christine Lalla/Watts Publishing p24; Lester Lefkowitz/Getty Images p25
The Publisher would like to thank Nigel Chell, Peter Higton,
and all at JCB for their help in producing this book.

Every attempt has been made to clear copyright.
Should there be any inadvertent omission please
apply to the publisher for rectification.

>Contents

My dump truck and me

Hello! I am a dump truck driver.
This is the dump truck I drive.

My dump truck carries soil, sand, rubble, and rocks on a construction site.

Dump truck power

All the parts of my dump truck are worked by the engine.

The engine is under the hood.

The engine is big and powerful.

◀ The engine needs fuel to work. Fuel is kept in the fuel tank.

Fuel is poured in here.

Wheels and tyres

My dump truck has six big wheels. They let me drive over rough and muddy ground.

▲ *The wheels are nearly as tall as me!*

◀ *The tires have a chunky pattern. This makes them grip the mud.*

The tipper body

I carry soil, sand, rubble, and rocks in the tipper body.

The tipper body is made of tough steel.

There is a big hinge at the front of the tipper body.

The hinge lets the dump truck turn sharp corners.

hinge

Tipper rams

There is a powerful ram on each side of the tipper body.

This is one of the rams.

The rams tip up
the body to empty it.

➤In my cab

I drive the dump truck from the cab.
The cab keeps me warm and dry.

cab

> I have a comfortable seat to sit on.

< There are strong bars behind the cab. They stop rocks from hitting the window.

Cab controls

I drive the dump truck with levers, pedals, and switches.

There is a camera at the back of the truck.

◁ *This camera shows me what is behind the truck.*

Carrying soil

Today I am moving a heap of soil from place to place.

A digger loads the soil onto the tipper body.

▽ *Now I am carrying the load of soil across the muddy construction site.*

> Dumping out

Now it is time to
dump out all the soil.

*I pull a lever to
make the body tilt up.*

When the body is tilted right up, the soil slides out.

Now I drive forward and lower the body again.

More dump trucks

Here are some more
dump trucks that I drive.

*I use this dump truck to
move rocks, sand, and rubble
on a small construction site.*

▲ *This giant dump truck could carry a whole house!*

Drive a dump truck

It takes a lot of practice
to be a dump truck driver.

*You have to learn how
to drive the truck safely
over bumpy ground.*

You have to learn how to dump soil in the right place.

You have to learn about all the dump truck's levers, pedals, and switches.

27

Dump truck parts

cab

ram

tipper body

mirror

light

hood

fuel tank

wheel

Word bank

construction site—the place where a building is built

engine—the part of a dump truck that makes it move

fuel—the liquid that burns inside the drump truck's engine to make it work

hinge—the pieces of metal that join the cab to the tipper body so that the truck can bend in the middle

ram—a machine that pushes and pulls

rubble—pieces of stone

steel—a very strong metal

Websites

The dump truck used in this book is made by JCB. JCB makes other kinds of construction vehicles, too, including diggers and loaders. You can log on to its special children's website at www.jcb.com/jcbjunior

> Index